Dadaist and Dada That

Critical praise for Djelloul Marbrook's poetry

Lying Like Presidents: New & Selected Poems, 2001-2020

Djelloul Marbrook's poems have been described by Edward Hirsch as having "the energy of a young poet with the wisdom of long experience." Over the years, Marbrook has mastered a warmly colloquial voice—the poems feel near and dear as an old friend speaking—delivering the philosophical ruminations of a life rich in experience and wonder. His poems feel as connected as charms on a weighty silver necklace from an older country, passed down from the grandmothers. They shine with honest hope. The last line of this poem could be the anthem of 2020. And they're also funny. "I am used to being old" carries no whine or chagrin. It's just true.

—Naomi Shihab Nye, *New York Times Magazine*

Far from Algiers

.. as succinct as most stanzas by Dickinson… an unusually mature, confidently composed first poetry collection.

—Susanna Roxman, author of *Crossing the North Sea*, in *Prairie Schooner*

... brings together the energy of a young poet with the wisdom of long experience.

—Edward Hirsch, Guggenheim Foundation

… honors a lifetime of hidden achievement… a voice that belongs to the vulnerable and exiled part of all of us.

—Toi Derricotte, 2007 Wick Award judge, co-founder of Cave Canem, author of *Tender* and *The Undertaker's Daughter*

... wise and flinty poems outfox the furies of exile, prejudice, and longing... a remarkable and distinctive debut.

—Cyrus Cassells, Nat'l Poetry Series winner

Brushstrokes and glances

Whether it is commentary on state power, corporate greed, or the intensely personal death of a loved one, Djelloul Marbrook is clear sighted, eloquent, and precise. As the title of the collection suggests, he uses the lightest touch, a collection of fragments, brushstrokes and glances, to fashion poems that resonate with truth and honesty.

—Phil Constable, *New York Journal of Books*

…delicately wrought… highly recommended reading… because, ultimately, this witness so clearly loves his subject.

—Eileen Tabios, editor, *Galatea Resurrects*

… looks at art the way a drinker drinks—deeply, passionately, and desperately, as if his life depended on it … makes you want to run out to your favorite museum and look again, as you have never looked before, until the lights go out.

—Barbara Louise Ungar, author of *Thrift; Charlotte Bronte, You Ruined My Life; The Origin of the Milky Way*

… one of those colossal poets able to bridge worlds—poetry and art, heart and mind—with rare wit, grace, and sincerity; a soft-spoken artist with the courage to face the "fatal beckoning" of his muse … crisp intellect, seamlessly interwoven with loss and longing. … poetry at its best: at once both gritty and refined, private and political, tender and tough as iron … well worth reading.

—Michael Meyerhofer, author of *What to do if you're buried alive, Damnatio Memoriae, Blue Collar Eulogies*

Brash Ice

… a precision that occasionally recalls Yeats …

—James Polk, *The Country and Abroad*

… aesthetically pleasing, thematically intriguing …

—Michael Young, in *The Poetry;* author of *The Beautiful Moment of Being Lost, Living in the Counterpoint, Transcriptions of Daylight & Because the Wind Has Questions*

Riding Thermals to Winter Grounds

… some very powerful lines, such as: "And then, near the end of my life, I became the man I wanted to be without the fuss and bother of giving a damn."

—Sidney Grayling, editor, Onager Editions

The Seas Are Dolphins' Tears

A 21st-century Blake—reconciling innocence and experience—Marbrook urges the contemporary reader to retreat to the quiet of unknowing, to live "in dusks of mirrors," where our truest selves can find their reflections.

—Dean Kostos, Benjamin Saltman Award for *This Is Not a Skyscraper*

I don't know anyone else whose writing increases in agility and breadth over time as his does.

—Lee Gould, editor, *La Presa,* the Embajadoro Press poetry journal.

Critical praise for Djelloul Marbrook's fiction

Guest Boy: Book 1, Light Piercing Water trilogy

What Marbrook does so well in *Guest Boy* is the contradictory elegance he showed in *Saraceno.* He finds the tender and poetic heart of very tough men. In *Saraceno,* it was low-level mobsters; in *Guest Boy,* it's men of the sea. They're a horny-handed bunch, and Marbrook's familiarity with ships and the characters of mean-street ports is deep and exciting. But Marbrook knows that these guys have a lot more going on within, and are simultaneously deeply tender philosophers. It's a mesmerizing book… You'll find yourself thinking about it long after you've finished reading.

—Dan Baum, author of *Gun Guys*: *A Road Trip*; *Nine Lives: Mystery, Magic, Death and Life in New Orleans*; *Smoke & Mirrors: The War on Drugs and the Politics of Failure.*

Guest Boy is a complex work: deep, passionate, exciting and beautifully written with flashbacks and imagery merging real and surreal. By opening up routes to the culture and history of the Arab world, *Guest Boy* helps us understand that world and our own.

—Sanford Fraser, author of *Tourist* and *Among Strangers I've Known All My Life*

… it is in books like this that I seek answers and guidance as I travel my own path to enlightenment and contentment. This book opened a struggle in me…

—Isla McKetta, editor, *A Geography of Reading*

Artemisia's Wolf
(in *A Warding Circle: New York Stories*)

Djelloul Marbrook's impressive novella . . . successfully blends humor and satire (and perhaps even a touch of magic realism) into its short length . . . an engrossing story, but what might strike the reader most throughout the book is its infusion of breathtaking poetry ... a stunning rebuke to notoriously misogynist subcultures like the New York art scene, showing us just how hard it is for a young woman to be judged on her creative talent alone.

—Tommy Zurhellen, *Hudson River Valley Review*, author of *Nazareth, North Dakota; Apostle Islands;* & *Armageddon, Texas*

. . lets his powerful imagination run wild, leading the fiction into unexpected corners where weird performers hold court and produce endings that both astonish and are frequently magical.

—**James Polk,** in *The Country and Abroad*; former contributing editor to *Art/World*

Saraceno

… a good ear for crackling dialogue ... I love Marbrook's crude, raw music of the streets. The notes are authentic and on target ...

—Sam Coale, *The Providence* (RI) *Journal*

Djelloul Marbrook writes dialogue that not only entertains with an intoxicating clickety-clack, but also packs a truth about low-life mob culture "The Sopranos" only hints at. You can practically smell the anisette and filling-station coffee.

—Dan Baum, author of *Gun Guys: A Road Trip*, *Nine Lives: Mystery, Magic, Death and Life in New Orleans*, and others

... an entirely new variety of gangster tale ... a Mafia story sculpted with the most refined of sensibilities from the clay of high art and philosophy ... the kind of writer I take real pleasure in discovering . . . a mature artist whose rich body of work is finally coming to light.

—Brent Robison, publisher, Bliss Plot Press; editor, *Prima Materia*

The Pain of Wearing Our Faces
(in *Mean Bastards Making Nice*)

I love it. I admire it. It is you at your best.

—Gail Godwin, novelist

Alice Miller's Room
(in *Making Room: Baltimore Stories*)

This enchanting novella is a delicately wrought homage to Jung's famous principle of meaningful coincidence.

—*Breakfast All Day*, UK

… the story draws us into that mysterious and terrifying realm where the heart will have its say and all who enter leave transformed…

—Dr. Patricia L. Divine, recipient of the national Head Start lifetime service award

Dadaist and Dada That

Dadaist and Dada That

poems by
Djelloul Marbrook

LEAKY BOOT PRESS

Dadaist and Dada That
poems by Djelloul Marbrook

"I've killed the other pronouns" first appeared in
Maintenant No. 11, June 2017.
"Mouseprint" first appeared in
Maintenant, No. 10, May 2016.
"The woven world" first appeared in
Sunflower Collective, August 2015.

First published in 2022 by Leaky Boot Press
ISBN: 978-1-909849-85-3

Copyright © 2022 Djelloul Marbrook

Djelloul Marbrook's right to be identified as the author of this work has been asserted by the author in accordance with the Copyright, Design and Patent Act 1988.
All rights reserved.

This book, or any part thereof, may not be reproduced, stored in or introduced into a retrieval system, or transmitted, in any form or by any means, electronic, mechanical, photocopying, recording or otherwise, without the prior written permission of the publisher.

This book is a work of fiction and, except in the case of historical facts, any resemblance to actual persons, living or dead, is purely coincidental.

A full CIP record for this book is available from the British Library in the UK and from the Library of Congress in the USA.

No part of this book may be reproduced
or transmitted in any form or by any means,
electronic, mechanical, photocopying, recording,
or otherwise, without prior written permission
of the author.

"With the sound of gusting wind in the branches of the language trees of Babel, the words gave way like leaves, and every reader glimpsed another reality hidden in the foliage."

—Andrei Codrescu,
The Posthuman Dada Guide: Tzara & Lenin Play Chess

For Darya Marbrook Miller,
my much loved Dadaist daughter.

Author's acknowledgments

Endless thanks are owed to my wife, Marilyn, who has in so many ways made all my work possible; to James Goddard, my publisher, whose steadfast faith in my work brought it to light and buoyed me in rough waters; to Sebastien Doubinsky, who published my work and introduced me to James Goddard; to Toi Derricotte, whose selection of Far from Algiers for the Stan and Tom Wick Poetry Award gave me confidence to continue; to Brent Robison, who published my first fiction and whose wizardly videos and deft hand with e-books still astonish us; to Kevin Swanwick, whose radiance as a reader and advisor unfailingly enlightens me, and to Emily Brooks, whose artistic taste, good cheer and resourcefulness seem fathomless.

Contents

Proem
    I've killed the other pronouns   21

What he told the arson squad
    What he told the arson squad   25
    Dadaist & Dada that   26
    The crack you pried   27
    Stop   28
    Antique light   29
    Probably an Istanbul   31
    Once ignoble   32
    Presently in her bath   33
    Hudson, New York   34
    Untoward dye   35

Dying to be touched   37
    Dying to be touched   39
    Mouseprint   40
    In a barbarity of roses   41
    Bare spot   42
    Fields of yellow cellos   43
    After vortices   44
    Djinn of salt air   45

Pee	46
Looking up	47
Melting on the floor	48
The door	49
The bathroom door	50

Painting with both hands

Painting with both hands	53
Moving away	54
Gehenna	55
Shipworm *(Teredo navalis)*	*56*
String of malice	57

Amplitudhedron

Amplitudhedron	61
Whirligig	62
Lost curators	63
I am the music of the place	64
Lavdrim Cami	65
Borrowed time	66
I am not but for you	67
Jigging the halo	68

The ringing crystal

The ringing crystal	71
Urns	72
I kissed Jane Avril's toe	73
The scent of a refrain	74
Night	76
Bedouin girls	77
Check all	78

Where these hands have been

Where these hands have been	81
Fatal pompoir	82
Overlong	83
Don't touch it	84
Seven potted ferns	85
Alembics	86
Thrilling	87
The woven world	88
Dave Wayland	89
Burnished shabtis	90

Zero is my god

Zero is my god	93
Mary Corbett's lips	95
The urn	96
Erasure	97
Desperate barista	98
Planning ahead	99
Heartburn	100
Mars	101
Just so you know	102

Cooper Union

New Lots	105
Valois queens	107
Impenetrables	108
Disdain	109
Harsh observers	110
It takes a year	111
About excellence	112

A certain actor's face	113
Solitaire	114
Cooper Union	115
Amnesiologist	117

Coda

Listening to the wind	121
About the author	123
A message from the author	124
Books by Djelloul Marbrook	125

Proem

I've killed the other pronouns

Don't tell me about your apps,
this tune's not in them,
and if I don't get it right
I'm going straight to hell,
which in my case is the sty
of unwelcome in your eye.

You are the second person who—
at this point anything applies.
I've killed the other pronouns,
I could say for a greater good,
but that would be a lie,
I killed them to address
myself to larger matters
than their parameters allowed.

How could the numen in my head
tumble into a culvert bleeding
and me not know it? Who
was that negligent me not
to notice I had no company
on the path? Surely I & they
distracted him from you
and thought himself whole
while being halved along the way.

We lose melodies in the snow,
we drop them into the sea,
they spin down storm drains,
flutter off cliffs, scrub, wear,
scratch away, and then when
a crack in the pavement
or smiling face hovers into view

they return as if someone we loved
had just taught them to us, had just
fondly touched our faces, blown
us a kiss, and that is baptism,
new purpose if only to put
one foot in front of the other.
Hell is putting by too well.

What he told the arson squad

What he told the arson squad

He didn't really want to get up.
The doorknob came off in his hand.
When he flushed the toilet the house blew up.

We're an invasive species,
he told the arson squad.
Like starlings, loosestrife and birdsfoot trefoil,
we indicate stress.
We are too much and too many
and recognize no neighborhood.
If allowed to get our rest
we turn good ideas into bombs.

If you let me sit awhile
I'll pass a hot needle through a rolled-up rubber band;
to save the world
from people like me. You of course,
you are your own threat.

Dadaist & Dada that

The only scents I have to make
should be intoxicating,
but first we need your insurance data.
Your life as a mockingbird is over,
you've run out of shrubbery.
You're only humanoid,
that's as far as we can go,
that's as far as we can take it.
Polyurethane decisions with conviction,
keep the surfaces clean. Success
is the best you can hope for,
but we are unable to guarantee at this time
that you will recognize it
and we don't know yet
if graphene will tarnish.
That's the problem with investment,
and then there are the fees.
Listen, Dude, it's always half-past something
you can't identify, but suck on this:
I don't give a shit, because all that makes scents
is too flagrant to breathe—
the Dadaist conundrum.

The crack you pried

And then I saw six other selves
dressed for six occasions,
unaware of me, intent
on what I might not approve.

The statue people in Central Park,
bedizened in bird shit,
painted over, never blink,
nor do my selves inviting me

to wait elementals' tables
in the rain, as I used to do,
while they conduct my business
in the plate-glass cruelties of the world.

Show no fear of not seeing us again,
they said, leave, be practical.
We have an agenda, we just want you to see
the many-sidedness of things,

The crack you pried, the certainty you're not
the damned fool you've played,
the certainty you're in, have always been
in the company of angels.

Stop

Viewer discretion is never advised,
not unless you're just fooling around.
Strong sexual content is a non sequitur.
So how do we start to live
when we've dispensed with the bullshit?
Just between us eels and oysters,
who gives a damn what's going on
the picturesque surface of things
where everything's a matter of perspective
and shipworms are disrespected?
Mute, delete, list, exit, record,
and of the symbols worship
the speaker crossed out, the sublime
stop which, though impossible,
sometimes invites us to hope.

Antique light

Hooyah, you're your epiphanies,
I wanna borrow you,
you gotta light the way,
can I count on you?

Me, I'm a hologram,
a projection hoo,
who projected me?
Yoo-hoo, listen t'me.

Does it matter,
are you madder
than when I said
I wanna borrow you?

Hoo, hoo, someone else
upon whom (dig it?) my light
has not yet fallen,
nor my darkness settled?

Each key's got a different sound,
each digit's ragged differently.
A piano has eighty-eight keys,
eighty-eight pianos don't sound the same.

No rods and cones assume
the same geometry,
and societies are arranged
to sap the awe from this.

Your epiphanies are your light,
too bright for some, calling
others. Nothing is the same.
I wanna borrow you

not because my light runs thin,
but to paint a certain wall
with our silhouettes
backlit by antique light.

Probably an Istanbul

Sorry you've lost your bodies,
I told the severed heads,
but I'm lost myself, I said.
You've lost yourself? they said.
Yes, it could be put that way.

Careful not to step on them,
I picked my way through alleys
til I found a convenience store
where I bought beer and chips.

Who was there to tell this to?
It was already slipping out of mind
like sundries I was bound to have been,
and if I had somewhere to go
it was probably an Istanbul
where I'd never been and was
being renovated for Russians
who'd moved in while the Turks
were stocking up the Parthenon.

Anyhow, that's how my mind spun
the few thoughts available to it
while my predicament
gathered overhead and I
suspected heaven might be
landscaped with severed heads
in burqas bewailing the fates
of damned brutal children.

Once ignoble

To have come to
to have become yourself
to have thrown out your baggage claim
to have let the muscle of your face
be still for once
in another's regard—
what championship
what acclaim
is as remotely fragrant
flagrant and subversive
as this?

You don't know I don't know
we don't know they don't know
but what is certain
because now you sleep at night
and what was once ignoble
is something else again.

Presently in her bath

Your skull is shining through,
wild roses in a bog, bones
revealing the original sketch
before experiences colored it,
stark as lightning gleam,
comfortable with creatures
not invited into the room:
specter come too soon, bottle
of ancient champagne in hand.

The hostess will be down presently.

Meanwhile, case the loot, sit here
by the fire, stop looking as if
nothing could ever warm you.
You'd rather follow me into the kitchen,
you'd rather have the maid
than presentlies and portent?
That's only natural for the half dead
who know living is a scam.
Fuck them, I know a crypt where we can party.
I've always tended to foreshadow
the fashions of next season, the mist
of words and their misdirections,
demeanor learned from films and friends,
peccadillos killing me. I'm not kidding,
Let's get out of here, the two of us
and the other two we're becoming:
white birch in a dark wood, swamp gas
and the beating of inhuman hearts.

Perhaps she'll drown in her bath,
presently in her bubbles of portent.

Hudson, New York

In a town like this, gorgeous self-absorption
blossoms in the cracks, unbolts and loosens.

People talk too loudly, they think to magnetize
is to enthrall, they leave no room for folk,
they leave us pooped, baffled, sad
not to have been noticed, glad
not to be like them. We experience
difficulty breathing, we're unsteady
now the storm has passed.
No one sleeps in such a town, sleep's
for suckers, losers. Winners
are always on high alert, wolves
with their snouts in the air, sniffing
forty times keener than human beings
for signs of envy and yearning, signs
we're tired, ready to fall down and be eaten.

In this town the honest tire too soon.

Untoward dye

Do the blinds despise the light
or do they habituate?
Pinholes punctuate the room,
but what was there to say?
Paintings sag on sketchy crutches,
books hurt and, yes, complain.

I am no more welcome here
than the marrow in my bones.

Does the TV meddle or only
its unfortunate colors? Am I
untoward dye in
a fabric-making or do the walls
protest having to make do
by jury-rig and perversity
with this slapdoodle, dawdling life?

Dying to be touched

Dying to be touched

to go on dying of it,
apocalypse surely
is contempt for now.
Goddamn the hole in it,
the imperfection,
whether it be love
or help held out,
goddamn it for being
too late too soon too
altogether trite.
Reel in with dismay
the illumined moment,
hold it in your hand,
then let it go
as you must be let go
and that is that and this
is more than its parts.

Mouseprint

Certain restrictions apply
when you live in an underwater town
hoarding air bubbles,
sending messages up
in burbles to the splitting light.

Life is low flight over reservoirs
studying street patterns
of drowned towns.

If your erection lasts more than four hours
consider the alternatives—
who knows what they are?

They'll put money in someone's pocket.

Earth is or is not a waterboard, after all,
but an insurance scheme, and death
is a dead-stick landing on water.

In a barbarity of roses

The good boy shut his mouth.
His nether parts gave up
their own manner of speaking
and he became a babel,
a toss of runes, a jam
to cryptologists, a solemn unworthy
better left to mower blades,
content to be a dandelion
in a barbarity of roses,
an invasive more familiar
than phragmites,
less truculent, more…
let's not loose a word here
that might obscure how subversive
these solarhedrons are.

Bare spot

I

Manhattan is the borough of impendingness,
line up to buy tickets, punch in at the ATM,
hail cabs, pretend to be preoccupied
on your cellphone, say hello to Paul Cézanne
who reminds there is plenty of bare canvas here,
but you are preoccupied and the crowd
is pushing you along, up escalators,
into elevators whose slapping cables you distrust.
Manhattan is the bureau of excuses
for all you ignored while you were waiting
for your turn with the cashier who ignored you.

II

City of cubes, city of looking out
and looking in, humanity en bloc,
city of shadow painters, blinding lies,
truths of naked chic, cardboard estates,
marble shanties, Zarathustrian city
where the fires are fed with currency
by the curators of the dead,
Braque and Picasso claim you,
but you remain Cézanne's bare spot.

Fields of yellow cellos

Lavender voice,
you could disappear just like that
mot juste in obsidian winter,
like that thingy there
sitting behind plate glass
in a witchy hat
yattering
like talons on a blackboard
& the diamond gong
in Alpha Centauri,
it could stop
deafening the amplitudhedron
& our tinnitus bow down to
fields of yellow cellos
playing my sympathies
or
just as plausibly tonight
a dirigible might dock
to the highest pinnacle
of my imaginings
& I might
exit through the wall,
blow the lamplights out,
finish
with Narcissus, having always been
suspicious of spring,
and with the faceless cartographers
& feathered conjurors of history
depart
for resurrections in the laps
of daemons.

After vortices

Okay, morning's more to pour the ash
—inbox, platitude, deceit—
from bridges I didn't cross,
more ash to pour, excuse,
a future in my mouth
I bargained for. Say it,
ash you bargained for,
and yes, I want a receipt.
Downriver I may need it,
you may need it
on some island past
Governor's & Verrazano,
past conceit,
where fourth persons live
of reconstituted ash
perhaps not my diatoms,
no, never mine,
I will be nevermine
in that old tomorrow
after vortices
not so much helplessness
as epiphany.

Djinn of salt air

I went to incomplete
majoring in poof,
divining truth
as a whiff of vermouth,
regarding sex as incalculus,
nothing meant to contain,
becoming a djinn of salt air,
metropolis my bellyache,
& then I was gone
not to know where,
frightened, too alive,
much too dead,
needing to be buried
not here or herein
but somewhere else
chiming like a bell-buoy
in the bay of yearning.

Pee

First we pee,
after that all sorts of good things may ensue.
The moon may dredge up the streets of drowned towns
as the reservoir falls and eagles snatch rattlesnakes
from islands made of drought. Better yet,
we have passed the toxins
left like underclothes by our dreams
and now our only urgencies
compel us to admire broken glass
in the curbstones of our dwindling ambitions.
We are dwindling, but first we pee
not to water black-eyed susans or the shadows
of cast-iron fences but to describe an arc
that nothing we leave behind
will speak better of us, and that,
that in spite of what you may think,
is a monumental thing.

Looking up

Every day somebody shits
on Beloved By All Who Knew Him.
Well, perhaps not on rainy days—little pooplets
not quite as perfect as goat beads but enough
to prosper buttercups and burn holes in snow.

That's how beloved he was.
Do you inspire such devotion?

It's probably one of five women he promised
to remember in his will. He died intestate,
he so resented the idea of dying at all.
And now he looks up at the bombardier.
not with the infernal grin of the dead
but with gratitude for keeping him alive.

Melting on the floor

All we look forward to bursts
in a moment's bubble, then is
revisionist history, snow
melting on the floor of the globe,
that waits to be shaken into flurries;
and what can we say about it
that is true, except it happened
this way and that, and one way
or another we made of it
what earth makes of snow,
clover does for soil, we gasped,
were never quite the same again
and had hellebore to look forward to?

The door

Here's what he was sad about
when they carried him out,
that the door still creaked,
but he was glad about
not being pissful any more.
And all the other urgencies
would settle into ground
like dew and as a genie
he'd be the fume of your bottle.

The bathroom door

You have to be bipolar
to appreciate a bathroom door;
it keeps the ignorant out,
the unenlightened.
Inside the illuminati
consider their options

and neither wail of sirens
nor importuning of phonies
prevail against the knowledge
all they want is control.
Exulting behind that door
is worth all that comes next.

No one outside wins
or understands.
This is the utmost church;
on the other side is heresy.
The heretics are sane;
God blesses this madness.

Painting with both hands

Painting with both hands

My mother painted with both hands
and loved the third sex more
than the other two. Her sinister side
remained enemies' propaganda
and anyone who saw her paint that way
or found her in bed with the other one
was lying and would have to be punished
with another painting hinting
at that third sex but denying
it was an androgyne. More likely
Bruno's triumphant beast
had impregnated her
with a little jongleur of galaxies.

Moving away

The ones we don't consult
from whom we move away
surface in drowning gasps
from our dreams, rippling
to the littorals of our minds
in shuddering circles
until we recognize
we have been reckless,
our careful planning cruel.
Improbables count.
The next thing we fix to do
is not as important as
people we don't consider.
None of us are casuals
but we easily become
each other's casualties.
The mourning detectives
we leave behind are sorting
evidence of our crimes,
and once in a lovely while
their suspicions subside.

Gehenna

The past is collage framed by our persuasions.
Outside on the street we pass as shadows,
stains, verbs of rain. The light in back of us
is a blood-moon thrum, something we must do
or be done by, tragic in its urgency,
unwarranted as climate, holy as itch,
too personal to belong to its carrier,
the antithesis of what can be contained,
meaning you in a raincoat, me refusing
to yank my stare back from the edge
of your prerogatives, a march of blanched souls
putting on a nativist show of belonging—
belonging is Gehenna under plate glass.

Shipworm
(Teredo navalis)

    Woodpeckers gobble the house again,
    vowels pecking at wormy consonants.
    Shimmering ribbons ward them off,
    but the house is crawling with ideas,
    an Afghanistan rich in rare elixirs
    that will ennoble elements if
    war lords and Talibanis concur
    that a future can be spelled in Kufic
    without American bodies, and poppies
    are evil's proper shroud. Summer
    shudders with the sound of beaks,
    guns feast on the heart of meaning.

    I don't believe the woodpeckers are evil,
    I believe consonants' strut offends them
    the way the existence of a boat
    offends *Teredo navalis* until
    he has digested it, and so the shit
    of woodpeckers will testify this house
    was full of ideas until a mindless savagery
    like Wall Street's ate it to the ground
    and it will be remembered as having been
    full of it, the way we and Talibanis are.

String of malice

She's a multiple impact bullet,
bound to do some damage,
strung not by Kevlar
but ignorant malice
shot through with beauty,
perfect hands attached
to an ogress's face.
Some before they learn to focus
toddle into her line of sight,
others must be stung by it
before she pulls the trigger,
before the chain shot shreds
the ether between you.

Amplitudhedron

Amplitudhedron

When I stroked the jewel of quantum physics I saw
a blue jinniyeh winding her tail
around the North Pole for leverage
as she diddled the clitoral seaway of Columbia
conjuring tsunamis of war.

I thought you were ambivalent about people, I said.
I am, but there are too many of them, she said.
Don't disturb me.
I stroked the amplitudhedron again
and the Great Lakes gave up
a world-befuddling fragrance
I knew would bear no good
for creatures who need to speak.

Since I suffer this impediment for what reason
am I given this privilege?

Did I ask you to speak? the blue jinneyeh said.
Voyeur me this, voyeur me that,

I have seen the fingers of the blue jinniyeh
postpone earthquakes
in consideration of larger events,
and in her sidelong, sidereal glance
I see that I am an essential flaw,
an indispensable facet
of an endlessly hospitable jewel.

Whirligig

Nothing but the horror of the naked moment—
society exists to spin the top and we
fly off it, sweat beads glistening
in the sun, ephemeral and wild,
splattering as we cathect
and running off to die out of sight
and mind—nothing but the horror
of knowing this is happening again.

We fly off the top but not the undersides
of the moment—they cling to rasp
the thighs of other dimensions and wave
goodbye to us as if we had been freed
from the revolutions of the orb, as if
somehow we had fled the whirligig,
as if its craze had earned it us
as its reward, and we are calibrated.

Each moment is a fathomless pit—
antigravity and antimatter sing,
but we fall back on the husks of old ideas
clapping our hands over our ears
and yammering about familiar things
because we fear the testimony of glass,
the second we will disappear,
and so we buy to bide our time on earth.

Lost curators

We're lost and mired in the cracks between
the doodads, gimcracks, gewgaws & baubles
we thought would make everything all right
and in that perpetual night we're swamp gas
fascinating the children who've ridden down
to the bog where the hellebore & skunk cabbage
shelter the elves who pee on our endeavors.
What we buy and curate fails to cure us
and we too settle in the corrosion and become
will-o'-the-wisp & purposes of unknown gods.

I am the music of the place

Illium, psyllium, do I look like I care?
The harum-scarums of Transylvania
I nightly visit and bloody-toothed
wake to vacant mirrors and confusions
owing to cavorting with the dead.
I've done this since adults warned me
to rein my glances in.

What secret underthings did they think
my look might rummage, what look
did they call a stare? Was it the one
that drew them in and left the room
empty of its props and prompts? Or
did it rearrange the furniture
of their settled minds and so disturb
the procession in duple time they called
a career, a marriage, a conviction?

I was too polite, but my nightly visits
to savage places sustained me.
Illium, psyllium, do I look like I care?
Yes, in my old age I think I do,
finally, and can't resist the hum of it.
My wife tells me to stop humming,
not to interrupt the music of the place,
but I am the music of the place
and that is what adults moved
heaven and earth to convince me
is a sin against the spheres.

Lavdrim Cami

Lavdrim Cami is pleased we're still alive.
Can you imagine,
considering the people who are not,
how a star or two might stutter?
He made a few repairs to our apartment,
a tall, grave man who dignifies
the people for whom he works. All is well.

Lavdrim Cami cares. That is how we survive,
randomness takes a geometric shape
and Piet Mondrian is absolved
of right-angle dogma. Natural geometry
is not as fearsome as classical design
as long as you do not insist on floors
beyond the threshold of your imagination.

My mother should have cared,
I should have cared about the old man
who asked me if I was god,
but it happened on Second Avenue
when my mind was settled on First
and it was too hot to think of anything
but the air-conditioning at Bed Bath & Beyond.

Why yes, I am, I could have said.
We could have spoken about why that might be so.
That might have been natural geometry,
but I was stuck on Mondrian and needed
a right angle to get there, that there
we always think we know.

Borrowed time

No, I didn't ask for a loan.
I have no plan in mind.
Keep your usurious terms,
collection agencies
and repossessors of lives.
I'm here to smell the flowers,
admire pretty girls,
listen to song and symphony,
visit museums, not debase
myself in your glass cage
or sell today for tomorrow.
You think you got mouseprint?
You shoulda seen my mother's.
Dandelions are worth more
than your promises,
they're my firmament. You?
You make poison mulch.

I am not but for you

You leave your footprint on my face.
Spin, whir, labels in the cabinet.
Medicines, make passages
through the cartographies of time.

Trace evidence, fingerprints, DNA
haunt the cosmographies of mind;
we are what has been left behind,
not pushing belongings in carts,
or wheeling our unbelongings away,
but following brush-choked ley lines
to personal Jerusalems
knowing what the tides scrub out
reappears in lengthened strides
leading us to uncanny salvages
from which we can't return
even when loved ones call us
from homes above the beach.

The evidence has carried us
to discoveries that were being made
when inquiring angels spun
the souls around
to impress them into the service
of fonder gods in better worlds.

Your footprints on my face,
the illumined, dervish lot of you,
are my glimmers and my glamors,
elixirs of my becoming.

Jigging the halo

I dreamed I lived an incident differently.
I would have had to be sober, alert,
less sunk into my coat and shoes,
and like someone beset with a halo
I said what I would have said
had I been grateful for the moment.
I dreamed I argued with the dream,
picked at its mortar, quarreled
with its improbability, but the halo
jigged impatiently, and I agreed
to what previously I disdained
because someone broke through time
to help me, to give me another chance
to be helped, and the least I could do
was to respond with a little grace
as if I had learned something
in the intervening years, something
about the rapture of the moment.

The ringing crystal

The ringing crystal

To reach the end of nothing, delete,
return, shift, command, learn
to solder your motherboard,
enter the workings of the machine,
remember no voyage ends,
we merely recompose, undo,
each of us a quintessential part
of a ringing crystal continuum.

Urns

I'm trained in the black figure technique—
I know what you're doing.
If I were a red figurist I'd play
whatever game would get me in
the temples and their patrons' homes,
but I have an obligation to the urn
and the ship in which it sinks
to be found 3,000 years from now
by someone who respects
what the black figures do
while red figures pour wine.

I kissed Jane Avril's toe

When I worked the formula out
I kissed Jane Avril's toe
knowing one of my drawings
drawn as well as a Lautrec hat
was whispering in the ear
of the detective on the case
and if that was not enough
to justify a life of doodling
what was and whatever it was
was not enough to concern me.

All that concerned Lautrec
offended his mother & all
that concerns me unerringly
finds the right people to offend—
odalisques of the harem
of a vampire or two but not me,
no, I am the gala material
of a Lautrec poster for a brothel,
or a brute café, the chalk & paint
of a poem without end.

The scent of a refrain

I've heard this refrain before,
cello, viola da gamba and drum,
not, I think, in this life,
perhaps among the Couperins.
What does it ask me not to do,
and if I hum it so well,
what's it calling me back to say?

I know life is pursuit,
tracking illumined footsteps
even when they stop at cliffs
and jump into the sea.

I know dogs have better noses,
wolves collaborate, and I
am too often distracted
by flora inappropriate
to the climate here, but never
once did I hold my nose
or shut my eyes, and that surely
must count for something,
like a melody assuring me
of having chosen well
at the last fork in the road,
the last precipice, the step
I called misstep that got me here.

I've heard this refrain before.
Surely the least I can do
is take note of it here and lift
my nose to catch its scent.

Cello, viola da gamba and drum,
aspen in an autumn breeze,
children playing, metal clanking,
wheel spinning,
and now the twinkling
of silicon and graphene.

Night

Night fills in the spaces,
gives the shadows
time to rest.

Night forgives the day,
night is charcoal,
original intent

underneath
the conventions
of the day.

Night is the canvas
on which we limn
the day,

etch the day,
etch ourselves,
fill ourselves in

and hope the colors hold
against the weathers
of our lives.

Bedouin girls

Bedouin bulbs—
tall girls taking
their roots with them,

tall girls swaying
in the fairy winds
of spring,

Bedouin girls
striking tents,
breaking camp,

sap returning
to the histories
of their feet.

Check all

Then delete. Everything disappears
but ghosts the machine. The ruthless finger
repeats the process in our sleep
but each dream mocks it. Delete becomes
paroxysm and uncheck all forlorn.
What is once seen changes us
and however much we cry undo,
rotate, insert and change the view,
a terrible witness is loose in the wiles
of circuitry and none of the beasts
in the bestiary are what they seem to be.

Where these hands have been

Where these hands have been

Do you know where these hands have been,
what they've done? These, those, his, hers,
theirs? The crannies they've pried into,
the interstices they've combed,
their particular rites, drugged, drunken, ecstatic nights,
bloodlettings, traceries on the wall,
obscenities and novas celebrated? How
can we live with such hands, how
can we live in such hands, eat from them,
accept their mercies, depend on them, worship them?
What do the cruel castanets say
in the flamenco of setting tables?
We should turn our eyes away
not to be beguiled by such capabilities.
We should refuse to be potter's clay.
Fat chance of that, nervous as we are.
What is the matter with us,
what is the alternative but to become vapor, fume,
shadow and spume, what can we do
about no perfect antisepsis being
to deliver us from the diseases of our hands?
What rings, bracelets and tattoos assure us
we are not about to die of secrets too numerous
to count, too much like keystones
to tinker, rebuff or remove?
They paint masterpieces, poison wells
and diddle the nerve-endings of the soul.

Fatal pompoir

The doctor who sticks her finger up your ass
should or should not be sitting in the front row
listening to you read a poem, depending
on the awful appropriateness of things.
That we eat meat, shit and fuck
but yet make such subtle art speaks to what?
I don't know, except the quandary is the cliff
from which we jump into angels' arms
wherein occurs the fatal pompoir
of our circumstance. Otherwise
what's there but speculation and tedium?

Overlong

Was it a mistake to live so long,
to burn so much carbon, to leave
too many footprints? How many
would have been appropriate?
I could have said enough, but I want
to suggest we have choices to make.
Long life may be a dodge, a delay
for which you reading this must pay.

Don't touch it

Take one in six for this and that
& other things

twice a day to pull
thoughts from each other's throats,

memories
out of the each other's pockets.

Take off your underthings
sublingually.

Shoot the breeze
with aspen leaves.

One in six to shut down Perseids
behind your eyelids when you can't sleep.

Be sure not to touch it
with your filthy hands

or you'll ride nightmares
back to mommy's barn.

One in six to separate
what you're doing from B-roll,

what you're shooting
from producers' expectations.

St. John's wort if you run out
naked to the streets

shouting, What, what did I do?
to a rising tide of applause.

What did you do
but despise caretakers?

Seven potted ferns

Seven potted ferns are having a thunderstorm
as they await their immigration
to a streambed sewn with blue sea glass.
Their papers are in order, they're not suspect.
In the house an old man in disorder
understands the purpose of lightning
is to illuminate what other kinds of light
disturb.

A clematis only lately dying makes plans
to listen to Couperin while drowsing
through the winter, sorry
only to have worried an old man
divesting his ambitions by humming in the dark.
How could these commotions
equal
blue sea glass?

Alembics

Damned if I know what's perfect
except that it would have killed me.
Aren't we divine imperfections
born to see what happens, born
to happen to it, not hapless, no,
but small alembics of awe?

Thrilling

I rode the tiger through the Milky Way last night
discussing William Blake—where do I get off,
Sirius?—thrilling to her musculature?
Forgiveness is irrelevant, I shouted to asteroids.
Will you get off it? she said. You? I asked.
Feel free, she said. What will happen to me?
What will happen if you don't get off?
But I'm thrilling to your musculature
and hope to see your green eyes again.
And will you clean my bloody teeth?
Thrilling to your musculature.
Are you mocking me?
I'm thrilling to your musculature.

The woven world

Unattainable inaccessible one,
we cast you out from within
only to feed on you like hummingbirds.

**

So he took a shit around noon;
where did he take it, why
are we always taking things?

***

Is acquisition scatological?
What's a thing worth but how
it's tagged? Tags are our obsession.

****

Fisheye, on your slab of ice,
is this about entertaining angels unawares,
or not?

*****

Stroke my face with rosemary,
soak my feet in sage; I will become
a thread of the woven world, a non-complaint.

Dave Wayland

How could he be gone?
I feel like Alexander's men.
The world will fall apart,
not into its constituent pieces
but flaming rags in a void.
Four ice cream trucks set out
to join the parade uptown
and he comes rocketing in a wheelchair,
throwing books and shouting
to his friends. I'm one of them.
I will go on. I will serve the Ptolemies
and other satrapies, bereft,
contemptuous of parades,
picking up the books,
trying to remember
what remains to do.

Burnished shabtis

Meteors travel eighty times faster than a bullet
and most of them are tinier than appleseeds;
imagine the size and speed of our thoughts,
imagine the meteor rain in which we live,
the divine bombardment we endure
to be the burnished shabtis of whom,
of what? What matters is imagining.

Zero is my god

Zero is my god

When I make two, a sad makeshift,
I'm lonelier than I was before,
because it stands against the one
they tell me gravity's for. They lie.
I am good at math. Zero is my god.
I am a hive of multiples, a swarm,
I have a secret that will burn a hole
in your pocket. Do you want it?
Not you over the counter, not you
pretending to love me, but you
wondering who the hell I am.
Listen, hand me your basketball,
close your mouth, stare at me.

I seed mountain freshets with sea glass,
plant succulents in stone warding circles,
leave urns in caves, inscribe rocks
with runes that speak in tongues,
dream of elementals in pavane
at these shrines, pray
to understand their kidnap
of my ordinary hours, fail
to see I've been carried away
and only pretend to live
among friends I hardly recognize.

I let my permission to remain
expire and wait for lightning to pry
the crack in which I'll disappear.
Now I wear the face of going,
my hometown of fear no longer
holds the back-alley horrors

parades of belonging deny.
I bled them out with staring.

Dogs see my shadow cross the ground
as a rabbit sees the hawk's.
Children hear my scream. I'm waiting
to ride a thermal above the hubbub
of trying to get along. Cashiers
struggle to make change,
glad to see me go.
I made the mountain strange,
a rightful priestess woken up
by the glamor of hoaxers.
I'm afflatus in a thrift shop,
turning around before gilt mirrors,
calling from the buried meteor
its sleeping illuminatis.

Mary Corbett's lips

The taste of russet apple and quince evoke
colloquys with the underthings of place,
rubbings, brushes, tussles, kisses.
Bell-buoys, train whistles, foghorns foretell
elementals we hope to leave behind.
The etheric between us ripped.
I didn't potshoot, snipe, or envy jadedness.
Everything promised to happen next.
But I had no ambition.
All I wanted was a world
that tasted like Mary Corbett's lips.
Encountering the incomparable,
I longed for the incalculable but found
only russet apple and quince.

The urn

Not if you were me. If you were me
I have no idea what you would do
except to notice women who walk like prows of ships
parting ether as if it were in their way,
men who have no sense of being noticed
and notice cracks in walls, weeds
in heroic places. If you were me
I'd rock gently in my shoes and stand off
for a tide or two. I'd listen
to ships passing, mourn bell-buoys,
gulls complaining. In my shoes
how would you proceed? Would you
sit here in this café and feel
your urn brim over with love?

Erasure

Bless me, Father, for I have sinned
all over the wedding gown
of a stranger in a parking lot
who may once have been my mother

and as if that were not enough
I have departed in peace once
too often for anyone's comfort
and no one believes me when I say

I'm going, except the one I just
darted into this dump to dodge.
What is worse than presence
or more sinned against?

I hurt for asking and wrong my feet
with choreography when
they know my compass swings
to more illumined things.

I am somebody else's body,
somebody else's blood, I am
wholly in communion
with chants of erasure.

Desperate barista

When will my hot chocolate be coming up
from the depths of the barista's despair?
No tip or whipped cream will repair
the tragedy my raring nostrils
have dizzied me on.
She and I share senses too keen for our own good,
hoping against hope that some good
will emerge from our graduate studies
in a certain kind of wolfishness that sends us loping
through our brambled dreams exhorting
ourselves to one more leap
over crevasses hidden under snow.
This is our snow, this casual social pact,
this conspiracy not to notice what we notice
bleeding out on ordinary day.

Planning ahead

Never did have a plan,
thought I'd miss too much.
Preferred my feet do the talking,
and when they got confused
I bought them a new pair of shoes.
I fell on my face often as not
and learned a lot about the grain of wood.
I finally found who I was
staring into puddles of water,
a celebrant of reflections, priest of ghosts,
unclubbable as I wanted to be.

Heartburn

Why do we call it heartburn
when we've had it up to here
with bile of memory welling
and the combustion of distrust?
I think lexicons and glossaries
are street signs turned around
to confuse retreating armies,
poisoned intel glistening
with malintent. What do I know?
I know I never met a name
that set quite right, perhaps
because I was born a foreigner,
more so to my place of birth,
so feelings would always seem
mistranslated, cockeyed,
made to be had up to here.

Mars

Does anyone remember living on Mars,
the oceans drying up and life compacting
into Hermes, Mercurius
and all that messenger ilk
we persecute for telling us
the last thing we don't want to hear?

You look as if you remember,
but you're going to walk out the door
before I can think of anything to say,
and that pretty much describes
life here on earth now that we must build
cities floating like lily pads,
alarmed as frogs.

Just so you know

More weird looks, acrid exudations.
Fall down, contraption,
be swept away!

Part, thin filament,
thing from they
who cling to this.

I don't care how you look at me—
I'm as imperturbable
as a poem.

Save it, you're going to need it
when your excrescences
jasmine up.

Don't bother me about the way
I bother you, I don't care,
my gravity's gone.

I just came here to buy some soup,
I shut the door against the draft.
Ring me up and let me go.

Don't encourage me to suspect
your jiggly memories go
into your condiments.

In my old age I'm short of patience
with ambivalence, and just so you know,
I don't like your face either.

Cooper Union

New Lots

When I dream of subway stations
they're cameras framing thoughts,
dioramas of poets and their poems—
Alexandria and Istanbul,
Cavafy with his friends,
Hart Crane building his bridge
between the senses and the mind.

I dream the mortal dream:
this is my last day among centaurs,
the first time I stay on to the end,
a certainty all these poets had
that each poem was their last.

The doors part, but I stay put.
I don't want to miss anything.
Auden waits at Astor Place
for the arrival of the logos;
I might be able to find it for him.

Rimbaud jumps the turnstiles
at 34th; I divert the cops,
so I miss the Guastavino stanzas.
Baudelaire, imagining women's jewels,
resents my notice; fuck him,
I'm going to reread Nerval
if my last day lasts long enough.

Mozart is orchestrating this,
them's the brakes, which this train
probably doesn't have. Who cares?
Poetry is a headlong thing,
each poem a murdered life.

I'm taking the Lexington Line,
changing at Nevins for New Lots
and my next life. Look for me
at abandoned stations, look
for my taxidermied ambitions
and maybe a line or two in tile.

Valois queens

She pins tatters of desperation in the air;
they turn to splattered glances and sting the eye.
Her three daughters bloom like black roses in snow.
She calls them ladies, these exhausting Valois queens.
Outside under August magnifying glass she catches fire
as the ladies groove around her, pissy with root beer.
This is how the world will end. No one will notice
except old men sitting in café windows wishing
they'd understood the terrors of motherhood,
understanding only understanding is too late,
hating the ladies for their beauty's costliness,
walking out without paying the cashier.

Impenetrables

You want to kill whatever's in there,
my sublime impenetrables,
you live to shake the box,
I live to keep it out of your reach.
Art is balm, love respite,
but I hear you in the woods.

Disdain

Hard to do nothing in a strait
because you're doing so much,
sweating out the vacuum,
wondering if silence is a friend.

Don't throw junk in the machine,
don't trash the ocean or mar
the sky with chemtrails
of your futilities, don't

insist something must be done
for fear it will be done and you
will like it less than this
moment inviting you in.

Your enemy is disdain
for what is happening now.

Harsh observers

Harsh observers of themselves, mad as hell,
the Stroller Nazis mow gaffers down
and animate their baby dolls,
and in their $14,000 Brioni suits four abreast
the Morgan Chase Hauptsturmfuhrers pretend
nothing's in their way but the husks
of their swindles, and all is well,
the economy is improving, ISIS is destroying
Palmyra, 60 Sutton has finally approved a flip tax,
and all the offending mirrors are being replaced
by complimentary copies of themselves.
How does a baby used as a battering ram
grow up? Does muscle memory recall
mommy's fury, and what was that about—
Dad's obsession with derivatives and receptionists?
Is life going to repeat that panzer thrust
through the innocent and infirm, or
will observation somehow shed light?

It takes a year

God wants him to be president;
what do the dandelions think?
My Apple's cracked, my Sony nicked,
the geometry of things is melting
in my hands, running through my toes
to the cracks in time and place.
If God wants him to be president,
what does it have to do with us?
Tell me, dandelions, I'm listening.
I'm going out on a limb on this:
our national security depends
on scaring ourselves to death.
I'd elect a man for saying that.
No matter how many times you behead them
they put their heads right back on.
Life's a damned lawnmower;
either we drink pesticide
or aspire to be dandelions
in spite of God's bad judgment.
What kind of world lavishes
money on tanks to think
and poison to kill dandelions?
I don't think he cracked my Apple
or nicked my Sony with his ambition,
I did that forgetting it takes a year
to revolve around a dandelion.

About excellence

The Austrian scythe and the Japanese gardening knife
glamor the barn with the sheen of purpose
but not like exhibitionists in a café.
They're about excellence, not the fear
of not having it, not the show of lack so deep
it rattles the tin ceilings of our nerves.
Outside life shudders with awareness of the blade,
hums and thrills with a question: what's too sharp?

A certain actor's face

If her face fails at being there
we suppose we know where there is.
If her mouth does not define itself
what is it we presume to know?
If her eyes retire like moray eels
must we brace for an attack?
What do we expect of each other
that speaks of what we lack?
Must we make someone whole?
If no one but ourselves
then to whom are we elusive,
to what end? To evade
the relentless mirror
that is the other's face?
Why should this one face
beg so many questions?
My grandeur's not what I know
but what I ask and answer,
though it prove the death of me.

Solitaire

So much finding a way
so much keeping away
so much keeping at bay
crosshatches on a table
impossible to varnish
Nazca lines imploring
the implacable rain gods
of a life ill-spent ignoring
vulcan truths up-turning
solitaires of the earth

Cooper Union

Hello, could I talk to you?

Coulda woulda shoulda,
do I have to answer yes or no?

I've been watching you.

Scratching the back of my neck?

And I think you're what it would be like
to talk straight and pay
profane consequences.

Which you look forward to paying?

Can you teach me how?

Lady, this is my stop,
this is where I get off.
I'd like to help you get off
on your magnificent question,
but it terrifies me.
I learned to talk straight
out of desperation.

I hear you. Your mouth is shut.
But I hear you. This is my stop too,
here with you. I saw you
back the bullying teacher down.
That's why I'm talking to you.
I heard you order him out of the room.
I was the one who applauded first.
You told him to come back when
he'd gotten over himself.
Then we all applauded,

all of us poor art students
whose free tuitions were cancelled
for the big shots' salaries,
we applauded you. Your mouth is shut
because you talk straight.
I want to know how.

You're gonna stand there till you make scents,
hoping I'll get drunk on you.
Want me to say that? Is that straight enough?
Ya think some of me'll rub off
and you'll get off on it cheaply,
get off on growing up on a Saturday afternoon
without leaving a tip,
not minding the closing doors,
or the sad baristas,
or the owners of the place
or the thugs on the platform
or the security cameras
or the men in black suits
or the sheer damn indifference of sunlight
or any of the paraphernalia
that keeps us from asking questions?

Teach you how I need transfusions
from djinn of salt air to sustain
the swagger of despair,
to walk another block, draw
another face? I don't think so.

But if you want to walk from Astor Place
to impale the sun on such a low ambition,
be my guest. I'm a sailor, I rock
because the street's unsteady
and nothing can be trusted to hold its shape.
Try emulating that, then both of us
can forget about closing doors.

Amnesiologist

We had to knock you out,
you made us laugh too much.
The famous poet snored at your reading,
hahaha, life is about his bum knee
and a good amnesiologist.
Your third eye popped in a sneezing fit
and you slurped eighteen oysters down
and quaffed Sancerre
rather than talk about it.
Besides, what was there to say
other than it drove you to suicide
and this is the hereinafter
whereinafter you studiously avoid
the rooms of your mind whose retinal readers
spit in your eye
when you play open sesame
and janissaries storm out of bottles
to snip your gewgaw off
in mid-sentence and prisons are privatized
to profit liars in their graves,
or something like that, who knows
the devil may care, but do you anymore?

Coda

Listening to the wind

Do nothing
and when the occasion arises
do nothing again.

What you want is trouble,
whatever name you call it.

Wealth is under your nose
but where is your respect?

Want only thisness in a thing.

Everything that refers to that
is an offense to this.

What is going to happen is made
of your observance of now.

Out of now is made
all that was given you
all it made of you
all you made of it
all you will leave behind.

Waiting for something to happen
offends what is happening. Worse,
you won't notice it when it happens.

There is no fresh hell worse
than waiting for it.

Who trained you to fear the doorknob?

Lift its prints. Nothing's something
more than it's ever been before.

About the author

Djelloul Marbrook's previous works have won critical acclaim and prestigious prizes, including the 2007 Stan and Tom Wick Poetry Prize, the 2010 International Book award in poetry, and the 2008 *Literal Latté* fiction prize. As a journalist, poet, writer and activist, he has invested his talent and intellect in an artistic voice exemplifying the best qualities of humanity. Through an engaging, well-reasoned and powerfully clear voice, he gives flight to a spiritual awakening and casts a wise shadow on the canon of American poetry.

—James Goddard, publisher

A message from the author

If you have enjoyed this book my publisher and I will be grateful if you'd leave a short review at *goodreads.com* and/or at the online website where you bought it.

Books by Djelloul Marbrook

Poetry

- *Far from Algiers* (2008, Kent State University Press, winner of the 2007 Stan and Tom Wick Poetry Prize and the 2010 International Book Award in Poetry)

- *Brushstrokes and Glances* (2010, Deerbrook Editions, Maine)

- *Brash Ice* (2014, Leaky Boot Press, UK)

- *Shadow of the Heron* (2016, Coda Crab Books - out of print)

- *Riding Thermals to Winter Grounds* (2017, Leaky Boot Press)

- *Air Tea with Dolores* (2017, Leaky Boot Press)

- *Nothing True Has a Name* (2018, Leaky Boot Press)

- *Even Now the Embers* (2018, Leaky Boot Press)

- *Other Risks Include* (2018, Leaky Boot Press)

- *The Seas Are Dolphins' Tears* (2018, Leaky Boot Press)

- *Singing in the O of Not* (2019, Leaky Boot Press)

- *The Loneliness of Shape* (2019, Leaky Boot Press)

- *Lying Like Presidents* (2020, Leaky Boot Press)

- *Dadaist and Dada That* (2022, Leaky Boot Press)

- *Once the Humans Are Gone* (2022, Leaky Boot Press)

Poetry and Fiction

- *Suffer the Children: Sailing Her Navel (Poems) and Ludilon (A Short Novel)* (2019, Leaky Boot Press)

Fiction

- *Alice Miller's Room* (1999, Online Originals.com, UK; reprinted as title story in *Making Room: Baltimore Stories,* 2017, Leaky Boot Press)

- *Artemisia's Wolf* (2011, Prakash Books, India; reprinted as title story in *A Warding Circle: New York Stories*, 2017, Leaky Boot Press)

- *Saraceno* (2012, Bliss Plot Press, NY)

- *Mean Bastards Making Nice* (2014, Leaky Boot Press)

- *A Warding Circle: New York Stories* (2017, Leaky Boot Press)

- *Making Room: Baltimore Stories* (2017, Leaky Boot Press)

- *Light Piercing Water* trilogy (2018, Leaky Boot Press)
    I. Guest Boy
    II. Crowds of One
    III. The Gold Factory

www.ingramcontent.com/pod-product-compliance
Lightning Source LLC
Chambersburg PA
CBHW022113090426
42743CB00008B/832